This Log Book Belongs To:

_____

Grateful

© Copyright 2022 -2030 All rights reserved.

You may not reproduce, duplicate or send the contents of this book without direct written permission from the author. You cannot hereby despite any circumstance blame the publisher or hold him or her to legal responsibility for any reparation, compensations, or monetary forfeiture owing to the information included herein, either in a direct or an indirect way.

Legal Notice: This book has copyright protection. You can use the book for personal purpose. You should not sell, use, alter, distribute, quote, take excerpts or paraphrase in part or whole the material contained in this book without obtaining the permission of the author first.

Disclaimer Notice: You must take note that the information in this document is for casual reading and entertainment purposes only. We have made every attempt to provide accurate, up to date and reliable information. We do not express or imply guarantees of any kind. The persons who read admit that the writer is not occupied in giving legal, financial, medical or other advice. We put this book content by sourcing various places.

Please consult a licensed professional before you try any techniques shown in this book. By going through this document, the book lover comes to an agreement that under no situation is the author accountable for any forfeiture, direct or indirect, which they may incur because of the use of material contained in this document, including, but not limited to, —errors, omissions, or inaccuracies

Date				Start Time				
Muscle Group				Finish Time				
Weight				Upper Body				
Lower Body				Abs				

Exercise	Sets	Set 1	Set 2	Set 3	Set 4	Set 5	Set 6	Set 7
	Reps							
	Weight							
	Reps							
	Weight							
	Reps							
	Weight							
	Reps							
	Weight							
	Reps							
	Weight							
	Reps							
	Weight							
	Reps							
	Weight							
	Reps							
	Weight							
	Reps							
	Weight							

Cardio	Duration	Distance	Heart Rate	Calories

Measurements

Neck	R Bicep	Chest	Waist	Hips	R Thigh	L Thigh	Calf

Note

Date			Start Time				
Muscle Group			Finish Time				
Weight			Upper Body				
Lower Body			Abs				

Exercise	Sets	Set 1	Set 2	Set 3	Set 4	Set 5	Set 6	Set 7
	Reps							
	Weight							
	Reps							
	Weight							
	Reps							
	Weight							
	Reps							
	Weight							
	Reps							
	Weight							
	Reps							
	Weight							
	Reps							
	Weight							
	Reps							
	Weight							
	Reps							
	Weight							

Cardio	Duration	Distance	Heart Rate	Calories

Measurements

Neck	R Bicep	Chest	Waist	Hips	R Thigh	L Thigh	Calf

Note	

Date				Start Time			
Muscle Group				Finish Time			
Weight				Upper Body			
Lower Body				Abs			

Exercise	Sets	Set 1	Set 2	Set 3	Set 4	Set 5	Set 6	Set 7
	Reps							
	Weight							
	Reps							
	Weight							
	Reps							
	Weight							
	Reps							
	Weight							
	Reps							
	Weight							
	Reps							
	Weight							
	Reps							
	Weight							
	Reps							
	Weight							
	Reps							
	Weight							

Cardio	Duration	Distance	Heart Rate	Calories

Measurements

Neck	R Bicep	Chest	Waist	Hips	R Thigh	L Thigh	Calf

Note	

Date			Start Time	
Muscle Group			Finish Time	
Weight			Upper Body	
Lower Body			Abs	

Exercise	Sets	Set 1	Set 2	Set 3	Set 4	Set 5	Set 6	Set 7
	Reps							
	Weight							
	Reps							
	Weight							
	Reps							
	Weight							
	Reps							
	Weight							
	Reps							
	Weight							
	Reps							
	Weight							
	Reps							
	Weight							
	Reps							
	Weight							
	Reps							
	Weight							

Cardio	Duration	Distance	Heart Rate	Calories

Measurements

Neck	R Bicep	Chest	Waist	Hips	R Thigh	L Thigh	Calf

Note	

Date				Start Time				
Muscle Group				Finish Time				
Weight				Upper Body				
Lower Body				Abs				

Exercise	Sets	Set 1	Set 2	Set 3	Set 4	Set 5	Set 6	Set 7
	Reps							
	Weight							
	Reps							
	Weight							
	Reps							
	Weight							
	Reps							
	Weight							
	Reps							
	Weight							
	Reps							
	Weight							
	Reps							
	Weight							
	Reps							
	Weight							
	Reps							
	Weight							

Cardio	Duration	Distance	Heart Rate	Calories

Measurements

Neck	R Bicep	Chest	Waist	Hips	R Thigh	L Thigh	Calf

Note	

Date					Start Time			
Muscle Group					Finish Time			
Weight					Upper Body			
Lower Body					Abs			

Exercise	Sets	Set 1	Set 2	Set 3	Set 4	Set 5	Set 6	Set 7
	Reps							
	Weight							
	Reps							
	Weight							
	Reps							
	Weight							
	Reps							
	Weight							
	Reps							
	Weight							
	Reps							
	Weight							
	Reps							
	Weight							
	Reps							
	Weight							
	Reps							
	Weight							

Cardio	Duration	Distance	Heart Rate	Calories

Measurements

Neck	R Bicep	Chest	Waist	Hips	R Thigh	L Thigh	Calf

Note	

Date				Start Time			
Muscle Group				Finish Time			
Weight				Upper Body			
Lower Body				Abs			

Exercise	Sets	Set 1	Set 2	Set 3	Set 4	Set 5	Set 6	Set 7
	Reps							
	Weight							
	Reps							
	Weight							
	Reps							
	Weight							
	Reps							
	Weight							
	Reps							
	Weight							
	Reps							
	Weight							
	Reps							
	Weight							
	Reps							
	Weight							
	Reps							
	Weight							

Cardio	Duration	Distance	Heart Rate	Calories

Measurements

Neck	R Bicep	Chest	Waist	Hips	R Thigh	L Thigh	Calf

Note	

Date			Start Time			
Muscle Group			Finish Time			
Weight			Upper Body			
Lower Body			Abs			

Exercise	Sets	Set 1	Set 2	Set 3	Set 4	Set 5	Set 6	Set 7
	Reps							
	Weight							
	Reps							
	Weight							
	Reps							
	Weight							
	Reps							
	Weight							
	Reps							
	Weight							
	Reps							
	Weight							
	Reps							
	Weight							
	Reps							
	Weight							
	Reps							
	Weight							

Cardio	Duration	Distance	Heart Rate	Calories

Measurements

Neck	R Bicep	Chest	Waist	Hips	R Thigh	L Thigh	Calf

Note	

Date				Start Time				
Muscle Group				Finish Time				
Weight				Upper Body				
Lower Body				Abs				

Exercise	Sets	Set 1	Set 2	Set 3	Set 4	Set 5	Set 6	Set 7
	Reps							
	Weight							
	Reps							
	Weight							
	Reps							
	Weight							
	Reps							
	Weight							
	Reps							
	Weight							
	Reps							
	Weight							
	Reps							
	Weight							
	Reps							
	Weight							
	Reps							
	Weight							

Cardio	Duration	Distance	Heart Rate	Calories

Measurements

Neck	R Bicep	Chest	Waist	Hips	R Thigh	L Thigh	Calf

Note	

Date			Start Time	
Muscle Group			Finish Time	
Weight			Upper Body	
Lower Body			Abs	

Exercise	Sets	Set 1	Set 2	Set 3	Set 4	Set 5	Set 6	Set 7
	Reps							
	Weight							
	Reps							
	Weight							
	Reps							
	Weight							
	Reps							
	Weight							
	Reps							
	Weight							
	Reps							
	Weight							
	Reps							
	Weight							
	Reps							
	Weight							
	Reps							
	Weight							

Cardio	Duration	Distance	Heart Rate	Calories

Measurements

Neck	R Bicep	Chest	Waist	Hips	R Thigh	L Thigh	Calf

Note	

Date				Start Time			
Muscle Group				Finish Time			
Weight				Upper Body			
Lower Body				Abs			

Exercise	Sets	Set 1	Set 2	Set 3	Set 4	Set 5	Set 6	Set 7
	Reps							
	Weight							
	Reps							
	Weight							
	Reps							
	Weight							
	Reps							

Date		Start Time	
Muscle Group		Finish Time	
Weight		Upper Body	
Lower Body		Abs	

Exercise	Sets	Set 1	Set 2	Set 3	Set 4	Set 5	Set 6	Set 7
	Reps							
	Weight							
	Reps							
	Weight							
	Reps							
	Weight							
	Reps							
	Weight							
	Reps							
	Weight							
	Reps							
	Weight							
	Reps							
	Weight							
	Reps							
	Weight							
	Reps							
	Weight							

Cardio	Duration	Distance	Heart Rate	Calories

Measurements								
Neck	R Bicep	Chest	Waist	Hips	R Thigh	L Thigh	Calf	

Note	

Date				Start Time				
Muscle Group				Finish Time				
Weight				Upper Body				
Lower Body				Abs				

Exercise	Sets	Set 1	Set 2	Set 3	Set 4	Set 5	Set 6	Set 7
	Reps							
	Weight							
	Reps							
	Weight							
	Reps							
	Weight							
	Reps							
	Weight							
	Reps							
	Weight							
	Reps							
	Weight							
	Reps							
	Weight							
	Reps							
	Weight							
	Reps							
	Weight							

Cardio	Duration	Distance	Heart Rate	Calories

Measurements

Neck	R Bicep	Chest	Waist	Hips	R Thigh	L Thigh	Calf

Note	

Date			Start Time	
Muscle Group			Finish Time	
Weight			Upper Body	
Lower Body			Abs	

Exercise	Sets	Set 1	Set 2	Set 3	Set 4	Set 5	Set 6	Set 7
	Reps							
	Weight							
	Reps							
	Weight							
	Reps							
	Weight							
	Reps							
	Weight							
	Reps							
	Weight							
	Reps							
	Weight							
	Reps							
	Weight							
	Reps							
	Weight							
	Reps							
	Weight							

Cardio	Duration	Distance	Heart Rate	Calories

Measurements

Neck	R Bicep	Chest	Waist	Hips	R Thigh	L Thigh	Calf

Note

Date				Start Time			
Muscle Group				Finish Time			
Weight				Upper Body			
Lower Body				Abs			

Exercise	Sets	Set 1	Set 2	Set 3	Set 4	Set 5	Set 6	Set 7
	Reps							
	Weight							
	Reps							
	Weight							
	Reps							
	Weight							
	Reps							
	Weight							
	Reps							
	Weight							
	Reps							
	Weight							
	Reps							
	Weight							
	Reps							
	Weight							
	Reps							
	Weight							

Cardio	Duration	Distance	Heart Rate	Calories

Measurements

Neck	R Bicep	Chest	Waist	Hips	R Thigh	L Thigh	Calf

Note	

Date		Start Time	
Muscle Group		Finish Time	
Weight		Upper Body	
Lower Body		Abs	

Exercise	Sets	Set 1	Set 2	Set 3	Set 4	Set 5	Set 6	Set 7
	Reps							
	Weight							
	Reps							
	Weight							
	Reps							
	Weight							
	Reps							
	Weight							
	Reps							
	Weight							
	Reps							
	Weight							
	Reps							
	Weight							
	Reps							
	Weight							
	Reps							
	Weight							

Cardio	Duration	Distance	Heart Rate	Calories

Measurements

Neck	R Bicep	Chest	Waist	Hips	R Thigh	L Thigh	Calf

Note	

Date				Start Time				
Muscle Group				Finish Time				
Weight				Upper Body				
Lower Body				Abs				

Exercise	Sets	Set 1	Set 2	Set 3	Set 4	Set 5	Set 6	Set 7
	Reps							
	Weight							
	Reps							
	Weight							
	Reps							
	Weight							
	Reps							
	Weight							
	Reps							
	Weight							
	Reps							
	Weight							
	Reps							
	Weight							
	Reps							
	Weight							
	Reps							
	Weight							

Cardio	Duration	Distance	Heart Rate	Calories

Measurements

Neck	R Bicep	Chest	Waist	Hips	R Thigh	L Thigh	Calf

Note	

Date				Start Time				
Muscle Group				Finish Time				
Weight				Upper Body				
Lower Body				Abs				

Exercise	Sets	Set 1	Set 2	Set 3	Set 4	Set 5	Set 6	Set 7
	Reps							
	Weight							
	Reps							
	Weight							
	Reps							
	Weight							
	Reps							
	Weight							
	Reps							
	Weight							
	Reps							
	Weight							
	Reps							
	Weight							
	Reps							
	Weight							
	Reps							
	Weight							

Cardio	Duration	Distance	Heart Rate	Calories

Measurements

Neck	R Bicep	Chest	Waist	Hips	R Thigh	L Thigh	Calf

Note	

Date		Start Time	
Muscle Group		Finish Time	
Weight		Upper Body	
Lower Body		Abs	

Exercise	Sets	Set 1	Set 2	Set 3	Set 4	Set 5	Set 6	Set 7
	Reps							
	Weight							
	Reps							
	Weight							
	Reps							
	Weight							
	Reps							
	Weight							
	Reps							
	Weight							
	Reps							
	Weight							
	Reps							
	Weight							
	Reps							
	Weight							
	Reps							
	Weight							

Cardio	Duration	Distance	Heart Rate	Calories

Measurements

Neck	R Bicep	Chest	Waist	Hips	R Thigh	L Thigh	Calf

Note	

Date		Start Time	
Muscle Group		Finish Time	
Weight		Upper Body	
Lower Body		Abs	

Exercise	Sets	Set 1	Set 2	Set 3	Set 4	Set 5	Set 6	Set 7
	Reps							
	Weight							
	Reps							
	Weight							
	Reps							
	Weight							
	Reps							
	Weight							
	Reps							
	Weight							
	Reps							
	Weight							
	Reps							
	Weight							
	Reps							
	Weight							
	Reps							
	Weight							

Cardio	Duration	Distance	Heart Rate	Calories

Measurements

Neck	R Bicep	Chest	Waist	Hips	R Thigh	L Thigh	Calf

Note

Date				Start Time				
Muscle Group				Finish Time				
Weight				Upper Body				
Lower Body				Abs				

Exercise	Sets	Set 1	Set 2	Set 3	Set 4	Set 5	Set 6	Set 7
	Reps							
	Weight							
	Reps							
	Weight							
	Reps							
	Weight							
	Reps							
	Weight							
	Reps							
	Weight							
	Reps							
	Weight							
	Reps							
	Weight							
	Reps							
	Weight							
	Reps							
	Weight							

Cardio	Duration	Distance	Heart Rate	Calories

Measurements

Neck	R Bicep	Chest	Waist	Hips	R Thigh	L Thigh	Calf

Note	

Date		Start Time	
Muscle Group		Finish Time	
Weight		Upper Body	
Lower Body		Abs	

Exercise	Sets	Set 1	Set 2	Set 3	Set 4	Set 5	Set 6	Set 7
	Reps							
	Weight							
	Reps							
	Weight							
	Reps							
	Weight							
	Reps							
	Weight							
	Reps							
	Weight							
	Reps							
	Weight							
	Reps							
	Weight							
	Reps							
	Weight							
	Reps							
	Weight							

Cardio	Duration	Distance	Heart Rate	Calories

Measurements

Neck	R Bicep	Chest	Waist	Hips	R Thigh	L Thigh	Calf

Note	

Date				Start Time				
Muscle Group				Finish Time				
Weight				Upper Body				
Lower Body				Abs				

Exercise	Sets	Set 1	Set 2	Set 3	Set 4	Set 5	Set 6	Set 7
	Reps							
	Weight							
	Reps							
	Weight							
	Reps							
	Weight							
	Reps							
	Weight							
	Reps							
	Weight							
	Reps							
	Weight							
	Reps							
	Weight							
	Reps							
	Weight							
	Reps							
	Weight							

Cardio	Duration	Distance	Heart Rate	Calories

Measurements

Neck	R Bicep	Chest	Waist	Hips	R Thigh	L Thigh	Calf

Note	

Date			Start Time		
Muscle Group			Finish Time		
Weight			Upper Body		
Lower Body			Abs		

Exercise	Sets	Set 1	Set 2	Set 3	Set 4	Set 5	Set 6	Set 7
	Reps							
	Weight							
	Reps							
	Weight							
	Reps							
	Weight							
	Reps							
	Weight							
	Reps							
	Weight							
	Reps							
	Weight							
	Reps							
	Weight							
	Reps							
	Weight							
	Reps							
	Weight							

Cardio	Duration	Distance	Heart Rate	Calories

Measurements

Neck	R Bicep	Chest	Waist	Hips	R Thigh	L Thigh	Calf

Note	

Date		Start Time	
Muscle Group		Finish Time	
Weight		Upper Body	
Lower Body		Abs	

Exercise	Sets	Set 1	Set 2	Set 3	Set 4	Set 5	Set 6	Set 7
	Reps							
	Weight							
	Reps							
	Weight							
	Reps							
	Weight							
	Reps							
	Weight							
	Reps							
	Weight							
	Reps							
	Weight							
	Reps							
	Weight							
	Reps							
	Weight							
	Reps							
	Weight							

Cardio	Duration	Distance	Heart Rate	Calories

Measurements

Neck	R Bicep	Chest	Waist	Hips	R Thigh	L Thigh	Calf

Note	

Date		Start Time	
Muscle Group		Finish Time	
Weight		Upper Body	
Lower Body		Abs	

Exercise	Sets	Set 1	Set 2	Set 3	Set 4	Set 5	Set 6	Set 7
	Reps							
	Weight							
	Reps							
	Weight							
	Reps							
	Weight							
	Reps							
	Weight							
	Reps							
	Weight							
	Reps							
	Weight							
	Reps							
	Weight							
	Reps							
	Weight							
	Reps							
	Weight							

Cardio	Duration	Distance	Heart Rate	Calories

Measurements

Neck	R Bicep	Chest	Waist	Hips	R Thigh	L Thigh	Calf

Note	

Date				Start Time				
Muscle Group				Finish Time				
Weight				Upper Body				
Lower Body				Abs				

Exercise	Sets	Set 1	Set 2	Set 3	Set 4	Set 5	Set 6	Set 7
	Reps							
	Weight							
	Reps							
	Weight							
	Reps							
	Weight							
	Reps							
	Weight							
	Reps							
	Weight							
	Reps							
	Weight							
	Reps							
	Weight							
	Reps							
	Weight							
	Reps							
	Weight							

Cardio	Duration	Distance	Heart Rate	Calories

Measurements

Neck	R Bicep	Chest	Waist	Hips	R Thigh	L Thigh	Calf

Note

Date			Start Time	
Muscle Group			Finish Time	
Weight			Upper Body	
Lower Body			Abs	

Exercise	Sets	Set 1	Set 2	Set 3	Set 4	Set 5	Set 6	Set 7
	Reps							
	Weight							
	Reps							
	Weight							
	Reps							
	Weight							
	Reps							
	Weight							
	Reps							
	Weight							
	Reps							
	Weight							
	Reps							
	Weight							
	Reps							
	Weight							
	Reps							
	Weight							

Cardio	Duration	Distance	Heart Rate	Calories

Measurements

Neck	R Bicep	Chest	Waist	Hips	R Thigh	L Thigh	Calf

Note	

Date				Start Time				
Muscle Group				Finish Time				
Weight				Upper Body				
Lower Body				Abs				

Exercise	Sets	Set 1	Set 2	Set 3	Set 4	Set 5	Set 6	Set 7
	Reps							
	Weight							
	Reps							
	Weight							
	Reps							
	Weight							
	Reps							
	Weight							
	Reps							
	Weight							
	Reps							
	Weight							
	Reps							
	Weight							
	Reps							
	Weight							
	Reps							
	Weight							

Cardio	Duration	Distance	Heart Rate	Calories

Measurements

Neck	R Bicep	Chest	Waist	Hips	R Thigh	L Thigh	Calf

Note	

Date		Start Time	
Muscle Group		Finish Time	
Weight		Upper Body	
Lower Body		Abs	

Exercise	Sets	Set 1	Set 2	Set 3	Set 4	Set 5	Set 6	Set 7
	Reps							
	Weight							
	Reps							
	Weight							
	Reps							
	Weight							
	Reps							
	Weight							
	Reps							
	Weight							
	Reps							
	Weight							
	Reps							
	Weight							
	Reps							
	Weight							
	Reps							
	Weight							

Cardio	Duration	Distance	Heart Rate	Calories

Measurements

Neck	R Bicep	Chest	Waist	Hips	R Thigh	L Thigh	Calf

Note	

Date				Start Time				
Muscle Group				Finish Time				
Weight				Upper Body				
Lower Body				Abs				

Exercise	Sets	Set 1	Set 2	Set 3	Set 4	Set 5	Set 6	Set 7
	Reps							
	Weight							
	Reps							
	Weight							
	Reps							
	Weight							
	Reps							
	Weight							
	Reps							
	Weight							
	Reps							
	Weight							
	Reps							
	Weight							
	Reps							
	Weight							
	Reps							
	Weight							

Cardio	Duration	Distance	Heart Rate	Calories

Measurements

Neck	R Bicep	Chest	Waist	Hips	R Thigh	L Thigh	Calf

Note

Date		Start Time	
Muscle Group		Finish Time	
Weight		Upper Body	
Lower Body		Abs	

Exercise	Sets	Set 1	Set 2	Set 3	Set 4	Set 5	Set 6	Set 7
	Reps							
	Weight							
	Reps							
	Weight							
	Reps							
	Weight							
	Reps							
	Weight							
	Reps							
	Weight							
	Reps							
	Weight							
	Reps							
	Weight							
	Reps							
	Weight							
	Reps							
	Weight							

Cardio	Duration	Distance	Heart Rate	Calories

Measurements

Neck	R Bicep	Chest	Waist	Hips	R Thigh	L Thigh	Calf

Note	

Date				Start Time				
Muscle Group				Finish Time				
Weight				Upper Body				
Lower Body				Abs				

Exercise	Sets	Set 1	Set 2	Set 3	Set 4	Set 5	Set 6	Set 7
	Reps							
	Weight							
	Reps							
	Weight							
	Reps							
	Weight							
	Reps							
	Weight							
	Reps							
	Weight							
	Reps							
	Weight							
	Reps							
	Weight							
	Reps							
	Weight							
	Reps							
	Weight							

Cardio	Duration	Distance	Heart Rate	Calories

Measurements

Neck	R Bicep	Chest	Waist	Hips	R Thigh	L Thigh	Calf

Note

Date				Start Time			
Muscle Group				Finish Time			
Weight				Upper Body			
Lower Body				Abs			

Exercise	Sets	Set 1	Set 2	Set 3	Set 4	Set 5	Set 6	Set 7
	Reps							
	Weight							
	Reps							
	Weight							
	Reps							
	Weight							
	Reps							
	Weight							
	Reps							
	Weight							
	Reps							
	Weight							
	Reps							
	Weight							
	Reps							
	Weight							
	Reps							
	Weight							

Cardio	Duration	Distance	Heart Rate	Calories

Measurements

Neck	R Bicep	Chest	Waist	Hips	R Thigh	L Thigh	Calf

Note	

Date				Start Time				
Muscle Group				Finish Time				
Weight				Upper Body				
Lower Body				Abs				

Exercise	Sets	Set 1	Set 2	Set 3	Set 4	Set 5	Set 6	Set 7
	Reps							
	Weight							
	Reps							
	Weight							
	Reps							
	Weight							
	Reps							
	Weight							
	Reps							
	Weight							
	Reps							
	Weight							
	Reps							
	Weight							
	Reps							
	Weight							
	Reps							
	Weight							

Cardio	Duration	Distance	Heart Rate	Calories

Measurements

Neck	R Bicep	Chest	Waist	Hips	R Thigh	L Thigh	Calf

Note	

Date				Start Time			
Muscle Group				Finish Time			
Weight				Upper Body			
Lower Body				Abs			

Exercise	Sets	Set 1	Set 2	Set 3	Set 4	Set 5	Set 6	Set 7
	Reps							
	Weight							
	Reps							
	Weight							
	Reps							
	Weight							
	Reps							
	Weight							
	Reps							
	Weight							
	Reps							
	Weight							
	Reps							
	Weight							
	Reps							
	Weight							
	Reps							
	Weight							

Cardio	Duration	Distance	Heart Rate	Calories

Measurements

Neck	R Bicep	Chest	Waist	Hips	R Thigh	L Thigh	Calf

Note

Date		Start Time	
Muscle Group		Finish Time	
Weight		Upper Body	
Lower Body		Abs	

Exercise	Sets	Set 1	Set 2	Set 3	Set 4	Set 5	Set 6	Set 7
	Reps							
	Weight							
	Reps							
	Weight							
	Reps							
	Weight							
	Reps							
	Weight							
	Reps							
	Weight							
	Reps							
	Weight							
	Reps							
	Weight							
	Reps							
	Weight							
	Reps							
	Weight							

Cardio	Duration	Distance	Heart Rate	Calories

Measurements

Neck	R Bicep	Chest	Waist	Hips	R Thigh	L Thigh	Calf

Note

Date		Start Time	
Muscle Group		Finish Time	
Weight		Upper Body	
Lower Body		Abs	

Exercise	Sets	Set 1	Set 2	Set 3	Set 4	Set 5	Set 6	Set 7
	Reps							
	Weight							
	Reps							
	Weight							
	Reps							
	Weight							
	Reps							
	Weight							
	Reps							
	Weight							
	Reps							
	Weight							
	Reps							
	Weight							
	Reps							
	Weight							
	Reps							
	Weight							

Cardio	Duration	Distance	Heart Rate	Calories

Measurements

Neck	R Bicep	Chest	Waist	Hips	R Thigh	L Thigh	Calf

Note	

Date				Start Time				
Muscle Group				Finish Time				
Weight				Upper Body				
Lower Body				Abs				

Exercise	Sets	Set 1	Set 2	Set 3	Set 4	Set 5	Set 6	Set 7
	Reps							
	Weight							
	Reps							
	Weight							
	Reps							
	Weight							
	Reps							
	Weight							
	Reps							
	Weight							
	Reps							
	Weight							
	Reps							
	Weight							
	Reps							
	Weight							
	Reps							
	Weight							

Cardio	Duration	Distance	Heart Rate	Calories

Measurements

Neck	R Bicep	Chest	Waist	Hips	R Thigh	L Thigh	Calf

Note	

Date			Start Time		
Muscle Group			Finish Time		
Weight			Upper Body		
Lower Body			Abs		

Exercise	Sets	Set 1	Set 2	Set 3	Set 4	Set 5	Set 6	Set 7
	Reps							
	Weight							
	Reps							
	Weight							
	Reps							
	Weight							
	Reps							
	Weight							
	Reps							
	Weight							
	Reps							
	Weight							
	Reps							
	Weight							
	Reps							
	Weight							
	Reps							
	Weight							

Cardio	Duration	Distance	Heart Rate	Calories

Measurements

Neck	R Bicep	Chest	Waist	Hips	R Thigh	L Thigh	Calf

Note	

Date				Start Time				
Muscle Group				Finish Time				
Weight				Upper Body				
Lower Body				Abs				

Exercise	Sets	Set 1	Set 2	Set 3	Set 4	Set 5	Set 6	Set 7
	Reps							
	Weight							
	Reps							
	Weight							
	Reps							
	Weight							
	Reps							
	Weight							
	Reps							
	Weight							
	Reps							
	Weight							
	Reps							
	Weight							
	Reps							
	Weight							
	Reps							
	Weight							

Cardio	Duration	Distance	Heart Rate	Calories

Measurements

Neck	R Bicep	Chest	Waist	Hips	R Thigh	L Thigh	Calf

Note	

Date		Start Time	
Muscle Group		Finish Time	
Weight		Upper Body	
Lower Body		Abs	

Exercise	Sets	Set 1	Set 2	Set 3	Set 4	Set 5	Set 6	Set 7
	Reps							
	Weight							
	Reps							
	Weight							
	Reps							
	Weight							
	Reps							
	Weight							
	Reps							
	Weight							
	Reps							
	Weight							
	Reps							
	Weight							
	Reps							
	Weight							
	Reps							
	Weight							

Cardio	Duration	Distance	Heart Rate	Calories

Measurements

Neck	R Bicep	Chest	Waist	Hips	R Thigh	L Thigh	Calf

Note	

Date			Start Time	
Muscle Group			Finish Time	
Weight			Upper Body	
Lower Body			Abs	

Exercise	Sets	Set 1	Set 2	Set 3	Set 4	Set 5	Set 6	Set 7
	Reps							
	Weight							
	Reps							
	Weight							
	Reps							
	Weight							
	Reps							
	Weight							
	Reps							
	Weight							
	Reps							
	Weight							
	Reps							
	Weight							
	Reps							
	Weight							
	Reps							
	Weight							

Cardio	Duration	Distance	Heart Rate	Calories

Measurements

Neck	R Bicep	Chest	Waist	Hips	R Thigh	L Thigh	Calf

Note	

Date		Start Time	
Muscle Group		Finish Time	
Weight		Upper Body	
Lower Body		Abs	

Exercise	Sets	Set 1	Set 2	Set 3	Set 4	Set 5	Set 6	Set 7
	Reps							
	Weight							
	Reps							
	Weight							
	Reps							
	Weight							
	Reps							
	Weight							
	Reps							
	Weight							
	Reps							
	Weight							
	Reps							
	Weight							
	Reps							
	Weight							
	Reps							
	Weight							

Cardio	Duration	Distance	Heart Rate	Calories

Measurements

Neck	R Bicep	Chest	Waist	Hips	R Thigh	L Thigh	Calf

Note	

Date		Start Time	
Muscle Group		Finish Time	
Weight		Upper Body	
Lower Body		Abs	

Exercise	Sets	Set 1	Set 2	Set 3	Set 4	Set 5	Set 6	Set 7
	Reps							
	Weight							
	Reps							
	Weight							
	Reps							
	Weight							
	Reps							
	Weight							
	Reps							
	Weight							
	Reps							
	Weight							
	Reps							
	Weight							
	Reps							
	Weight							
	Reps							
	Weight							

Cardio	Duration	Distance	Heart Rate	Calories

Measurements

Neck	R Bicep	Chest	Waist	Hips	R Thigh	L Thigh	Calf

Note

Date				Start Time			
Muscle Group				Finish Time			
Weight				Upper Body			
Lower Body				Abs			

Exercise	Sets	Set 1	Set 2	Set 3	Set 4	Set 5	Set 6	Set 7
	Reps							
	Weight							
	Reps							
	Weight							
	Reps							
	Weight							
	Reps							
	Weight							
	Reps							
	Weight							
	Reps							
	Weight							
	Reps							
	Weight							
	Reps							
	Weight							
	Reps							
	Weight							

Cardio	Duration	Distance	Heart Rate	Calories

Measurements

Neck	R Bicep	Chest	Waist	Hips	R Thigh	L Thigh	Calf

Note	

Date				Start Time				
Muscle Group				Finish Time				
Weight				Upper Body				
Lower Body				Abs				

Exercise	Sets	Set 1	Set 2	Set 3	Set 4	Set 5	Set 6	Set 7
	Reps							
	Weight							
	Reps							
	Weight							
	Reps							
	Weight							
	Reps							
	Weight							
	Reps							
	Weight							
	Reps							
	Weight							
	Reps							
	Weight							
	Reps							
	Weight							
	Reps							
	Weight							

Cardio	Duration	Distance	Heart Rate	Calories

Measurements

Neck	R Bicep	Chest	Waist	Hips	R Thigh	L Thigh	Calf

Note

Date		Start Time	
Muscle Group		Finish Time	
Weight		Upper Body	
Lower Body		Abs	

Exercise	Sets	Set 1	Set 2	Set 3	Set 4	Set 5	Set 6	Set 7
	Reps							
	Weight							
	Reps							
	Weight							
	Reps							
	Weight							
	Reps							
	Weight							
	Reps							
	Weight							
	Reps							
	Weight							
	Reps							
	Weight							
	Reps							
	Weight							
	Reps							
	Weight							

Cardio	Duration	Distance	Heart Rate	Calories

Measurements

Neck	R Bicep	Chest	Waist	Hips	R Thigh	L Thigh	Calf

Note	

Date				Start Time				
Muscle Group				Finish Time				
Weight				Upper Body				
Lower Body				Abs				

Exercise	Sets	Set 1	Set 2	Set 3	Set 4	Set 5	Set 6	Set 7
	Reps							
	Weight							
	Reps							
	Weight							
	Reps							
	Weight							
	Reps							
	Weight							
	Reps							
	Weight							
	Reps							
	Weight							
	Reps							
	Weight							
	Reps							
	Weight							
	Reps							
	Weight							

Cardio	Duration	Distance	Heart Rate	Calories

Measurements

Neck	R Bicep	Chest	Waist	Hips	R Thigh	L Thigh	Calf

Note	

Date			Start Time	
Muscle Group			Finish Time	
Weight			Upper Body	
Lower Body			Abs	

Exercise	Sets	Set 1	Set 2	Set 3	Set 4	Set 5	Set 6	Set 7
	Reps							
	Weight							
	Reps							
	Weight							
	Reps							
	Weight							
	Reps							
	Weight							
	Reps							
	Weight							
	Reps							
	Weight							
	Reps							
	Weight							
	Reps							
	Weight							
	Reps							
	Weight							

Cardio	Duration	Distance	Heart Rate	Calories

Measurements

Neck	R Bicep	Chest	Waist	Hips	R Thigh	L Thigh	Calf

Note	

Date			Start Time	
Muscle Group			Finish Time	
Weight			Upper Body	
Lower Body			Abs	

Exercise	Sets	Set 1	Set 2	Set 3	Set 4	Set 5	Set 6	Set 7
	Reps							
	Weight							
	Reps							
	Weight							
	Reps							
	Weight							
	Reps							
	Weight							
	Reps							
	Weight							
	Reps							
	Weight							
	Reps							
	Weight							
	Reps							
	Weight							
	Reps							
	Weight							

Cardio	Duration	Distance	Heart Rate	Calories

Measurements

Neck	R Bicep	Chest	Waist	Hips	R Thigh	L Thigh	Calf

Note

Date				Start Time			
Muscle Group				Finish Time			
Weight				Upper Body			
Lower Body				Abs			

Exercise	Sets	Set 1	Set 2	Set 3	Set 4	Set 5	Set 6	Set 7
	Reps							
	Weight							
	Reps							
	Weight							
	Reps							
	Weight							
	Reps							
	Weight							
	Reps							
	Weight							
	Reps							
	Weight							
	Reps							
	Weight							
	Reps							
	Weight							
	Reps							
	Weight							

Cardio	Duration	Distance	Heart Rate	Calories

Measurements

Neck	R Bicep	Chest	Waist	Hips	R Thigh	L Thigh	Calf

Note	

Date				Start Time				
Muscle Group				Finish Time				
Weight				Upper Body				
Lower Body				Abs				

Exercise	Sets	Set 1	Set 2	Set 3	Set 4	Set 5	Set 6	Set 7
	Reps							
	Weight							
	Reps							
	Weight							
	Reps							
	Weight							
	Reps							
	Weight							
	Reps							
	Weight							
	Reps							
	Weight							
	Reps							
	Weight							
	Reps							
	Weight							
	Reps							
	Weight							

Cardio	Duration	Distance	Heart Rate	Calories

Measurements

Neck	R Bicep	Chest	Waist	Hips	R Thigh	L Thigh	Calf

Note	

Date			Start Time	
Muscle Group			Finish Time	
Weight			Upper Body	
Lower Body			Abs	

Exercise	Sets	Set 1	Set 2	Set 3	Set 4	Set 5	Set 6	Set 7
	Reps							
	Weight							
	Reps							
	Weight							
	Reps							
	Weight							
	Reps							
	Weight							
	Reps							
	Weight							
	Reps							
	Weight							
	Reps							
	Weight							
	Reps							
	Weight							
	Reps							
	Weight							

Cardio	Duration	Distance	Heart Rate	Calories

Measurements

Neck	R Bicep	Chest	Waist	Hips	R Thigh	L Thigh	Calf

Note	

Date				Start Time				
Muscle Group				Finish Time				
Weight				Upper Body				
Lower Body				Abs				

Exercise	Sets	Set 1	Set 2	Set 3	Set 4	Set 5	Set 6	Set 7
	Reps							
	Weight							
	Reps							
	Weight							
	Reps							
	Weight							
	Reps							
	Weight							
	Reps							
	Weight							
	Reps							
	Weight							
	Reps							
	Weight							
	Reps							
	Weight							
	Reps							
	Weight							

Cardio	Duration	Distance	Heart Rate	Calories

Measurements

Neck	R Bicep	Chest	Waist	Hips	R Thigh	L Thigh	Calf

Note

Date			Start Time			
Muscle Group			Finish Time			
Weight			Upper Body			
Lower Body			Abs			

Exercise	Sets	Set 1	Set 2	Set 3	Set 4	Set 5	Set 6	Set 7
	Reps							
	Weight							
	Reps							
	Weight							
	Reps							
	Weight							
	Reps							
	Weight							
	Reps							
	Weight							
	Reps							
	Weight							
	Reps							
	Weight							
	Reps							
	Weight							
	Reps							
	Weight							

Cardio	Duration	Distance	Heart Rate	Calories

Measurements							
Neck	R Bicep	Chest	Waist	Hips	R Thigh	L Thigh	Calf

Note

Date				Start Time				
Muscle Group				Finish Time				
Weight				Upper Body				
Lower Body				Abs				

Exercise	Sets	Set 1	Set 2	Set 3	Set 4	Set 5	Set 6	Set 7
	Reps							
	Weight							
	Reps							
	Weight							
	Reps							
	Weight							
	Reps							
	Weight							
	Reps							
	Weight							
	Reps							
	Weight							
	Reps							
	Weight							
	Reps							
	Weight							
	Reps							
	Weight							

Cardio	Duration	Distance	Heart Rate	Calories

Measurements

Neck	R Bicep	Chest	Waist	Hips	R Thigh	L Thigh	Calf

Note	

Date			Start Time	
Muscle Group			Finish Time	
Weight			Upper Body	
Lower Body			Abs	

Exercise	Sets	Set 1	Set 2	Set 3	Set 4	Set 5	Set 6	Set 7
	Reps							
	Weight							
	Reps							
	Weight							
	Reps							
	Weight							
	Reps							
	Weight							
	Reps							
	Weight							
	Reps							
	Weight							
	Reps							
	Weight							
	Reps							
	Weight							
	Reps							
	Weight							

Cardio	Duration	Distance	Heart Rate	Calories

Measurements

Neck	R Bicep	Chest	Waist	Hips	R Thigh	L Thigh	Calf

Note	

Date				Start Time				
Muscle Group				Finish Time				
Weight				Upper Body				
Lower Body				Abs				

Exercise	Sets	Set 1	Set 2	Set 3	Set 4	Set 5	Set 6	Set 7
	Reps							
	Weight							
	Reps							
	Weight							
	Reps							
	Weight							
	Reps							
	Weight							
	Reps							
	Weight							
	Reps							
	Weight							
	Reps							
	Weight							
	Reps							
	Weight							
	Reps							
	Weight							

Cardio	Duration	Distance	Heart Rate	Calories

Measurements

Neck	R Bicep	Chest	Waist	Hips	R Thigh	L Thigh	Calf

Note	

Date			Start Time					
Muscle Group			Finish Time					
Weight			Upper Body					
Lower Body			Abs					

Exercise	Sets	Set 1	Set 2	Set 3	Set 4	Set 5	Set 6	Set 7
	Reps							
	Weight							
	Reps							
	Weight							
	Reps							
	Weight							
	Reps							
	Weight							
	Reps							
	Weight							
	Reps							
	Weight							
	Reps							
	Weight							
	Reps							
	Weight							
	Reps							
	Weight							

Cardio	Duration	Distance	Heart Rate	Calories

Measurements

Neck	R Bicep	Chest	Waist	Hips	R Thigh	L Thigh	Calf

Note	

Date				Start Time			
Muscle Group				Finish Time			
Weight				Upper Body			
Lower Body				Abs			

Exercise	Sets	Set 1	Set 2	Set 3	Set 4	Set 5	Set 6	Set 7
	Reps							
	Weight							
	Reps							
	Weight							
	Reps							
	Weight							
	Reps							
	Weight							
	Reps							
	Weight							
	Reps							
	Weight							
	Reps							
	Weight							
	Reps							
	Weight							
	Reps							
	Weight							

Cardio	Duration	Distance	Heart Rate	Calories

Measurements

Neck	R Bicep	Chest	Waist	Hips	R Thigh	L Thigh	Calf

Note	

Date			Start Time	
Muscle Group			Finish Time	
Weight			Upper Body	
Lower Body			Abs	

Exercise	Sets	Set 1	Set 2	Set 3	Set 4	Set 5	Set 6	Set 7
	Reps							
	Weight							
	Reps							
	Weight							
	Reps							
	Weight							
	Reps							
	Weight							
	Reps							
	Weight							
	Reps							
	Weight							
	Reps							
	Weight							
	Reps							
	Weight							
	Reps							
	Weight							

Cardio	Duration	Distance	Heart Rate	Calories

Measurements

Neck	R Bicep	Chest	Waist	Hips	R Thigh	L Thigh	Calf

Note	

Date				Start Time				
Muscle Group				Finish Time				
Weight				Upper Body				
Lower Body				Abs				

Exercise	Sets	Set 1	Set 2	Set 3	Set 4	Set 5	Set 6	Set 7
	Reps							
	Weight							
	Reps							
	Weight							
	Reps							
	Weight							
	Reps							
	Weight							
	Reps							
	Weight							
	Reps							
	Weight							
	Reps							
	Weight							
	Reps							
	Weight							
	Reps							
	Weight							

Cardio	Duration	Distance	Heart Rate	Calories

Measurements							
Neck	R Bicep	Chest	Waist	Hips	R Thigh	L Thigh	Calf

Note	

Date			Start Time	
Muscle Group			Finish Time	
Weight			Upper Body	
Lower Body			Abs	

Exercise	Sets	Set 1	Set 2	Set 3	Set 4	Set 5	Set 6	Set 7
	Reps							
	Weight							
	Reps							
	Weight							
	Reps							
	Weight							
	Reps							
	Weight							
	Reps							
	Weight							
	Reps							
	Weight							
	Reps							
	Weight							
	Reps							
	Weight							

Cardio	Duration	Distance	Heart Rate	Calories

Measurements

Neck	R Bicep	Chest	Waist	Hips	R Thigh	L Thigh	Calf

Note	

Date				Start Time				
Muscle Group				Finish Time				
Weight				Upper Body				
Lower Body				Abs				

Exercise	Sets	Set 1	Set 2	Set 3	Set 4	Set 5	Set 6	Set 7
	Reps							
	Weight							
	Reps							
	Weight							
	Reps							
	Weight							
	Reps							
	Weight							
	Reps							
	Weight							
	Reps							
	Weight							
	Reps							
	Weight							
	Reps							
	Weight							
	Reps							
	Weight							

Cardio	Duration	Distance	Heart Rate	Calories

Measurements

Neck	R Bicep	Chest	Waist	Hips	R Thigh	L Thigh	Calf

Note	

Date		Start Time	
Muscle Group		Finish Time	
Weight		Upper Body	
Lower Body		Abs	

Exercise	Sets	Set 1	Set 2	Set 3	Set 4	Set 5	Set 6	Set 7
	Reps							
	Weight							
	Reps							
	Weight							
	Reps							
	Weight							
	Reps							
	Weight							
	Reps							
	Weight							
	Reps							
	Weight							
	Reps							
	Weight							
	Reps							
	Weight							
	Reps							
	Weight							

Cardio	Duration	Distance	Heart Rate	Calories

Measurements

Neck	R Bicep	Chest	Waist	Hips	R Thigh	L Thigh	Calf

Note	

Date				Start Time			
Muscle Group				Finish Time			
Weight				Upper Body			
Lower Body				Abs			

Exercise	Sets	Set 1	Set 2	Set 3	Set 4	Set 5	Set 6	Set 7
	Reps							
	Weight							
	Reps							
	Weight							
	Reps							
	Weight							
	Reps							
	Weight							
	Reps							
	Weight							
	Reps							
	Weight							
	Reps							
	Weight							
	Reps							
	Weight							
	Reps							
	Weight							

Cardio	Duration	Distance	Heart Rate	Calories

Measurements

Neck	R Bicep	Chest	Waist	Hips	R Thigh	L Thigh	Calf

Note

Date			Start Time				
Muscle Group			Finish Time				
Weight			Upper Body				
Lower Body			Abs				

Exercise	Sets	Set 1	Set 2	Set 3	Set 4	Set 5	Set 6	Set 7
	Reps							
	Weight							
	Reps							
	Weight							
	Reps							
	Weight							
	Reps							
	Weight							
	Reps							
	Weight							
	Reps							
	Weight							
	Reps							
	Weight							
	Reps							
	Weight							
	Reps							
	Weight							

Cardio	Duration	Distance	Heart Rate	Calories

Measurements

Neck	R Bicep	Chest	Waist	Hips	R Thigh	L Thigh	Calf

Note	

Date				Start Time				
Muscle Group				Finish Time				
Weight				Upper Body				
Lower Body				Abs				

Exercise	Sets	Set 1	Set 2	Set 3	Set 4	Set 5	Set 6	Set 7
	Reps							
	Weight							
	Reps							
	Weight							
	Reps							
	Weight							
	Reps							
	Weight							
	Reps							
	Weight							
	Reps							
	Weight							
	Reps							
	Weight							
	Reps							
	Weight							
	Reps							
	Weight							

Cardio	Duration	Distance	Heart Rate	Calories

Measurements

Neck	R Bicep	Chest	Waist	Hips	R Thigh	L Thigh	Calf

Note	

Date			Start Time	
Muscle Group			Finish Time	
Weight			Upper Body	
Lower Body			Abs	

Exercise	Sets	Set 1	Set 2	Set 3	Set 4	Set 5	Set 6	Set 7
	Reps							
	Weight							
	Reps							
	Weight							
	Reps							
	Weight							
	Reps							
	Weight							
	Reps							
	Weight							
	Reps							
	Weight							
	Reps							
	Weight							
	Reps							
	Weight							
	Reps							
	Weight							

Cardio	Duration	Distance	Heart Rate	Calories

Measurements

Neck	R Bicep	Chest	Waist	Hips	R Thigh	L Thigh	Calf

Note	

Date				Start Time				
Muscle Group				Finish Time				
Weight				Upper Body				
Lower Body				Abs				

Exercise	Sets	Set 1	Set 2	Set 3	Set 4	Set 5	Set 6	Set 7
	Reps							
	Weight							
	Reps							
	Weight							
	Reps							
	Weight							
	Reps							
	Weight							
	Reps							
	Weight							
	Reps							
	Weight							
	Reps							
	Weight							
	Reps							
	Weight							
	Reps							
	Weight							

Cardio	Duration	Distance	Heart Rate	Calories

Measurements

Neck	R Bicep	Chest	Waist	Hips	R Thigh	L Thigh	Calf

Note	

Date				Start Time			
Muscle Group				Finish Time			
Weight				Upper Body			
Lower Body				Abs			

Exercise	Sets	Set 1	Set 2	Set 3	Set 4	Set 5	Set 6	Set 7
	Reps							
	Weight							
	Reps							
	Weight							
	Reps							
	Weight							
	Reps							
	Weight							
	Reps							
	Weight							
	Reps							
	Weight							
	Reps							
	Weight							
	Reps							
	Weight							
	Reps							
	Weight							

Cardio	Duration	Distance	Heart Rate	Calories

Measurements

Neck	R Bicep	Chest	Waist	Hips	R Thigh	L Thigh	Calf

Note	

Date				Start Time				
Muscle Group				Finish Time				
Weight				Upper Body				
Lower Body				Abs				

Exercise	Sets	Set 1	Set 2	Set 3	Set 4	Set 5	Set 6	Set 7
	Reps							
	Weight							
	Reps							
	Weight							
	Reps							
	Weight							
	Reps							
	Weight							
	Reps							
	Weight							
	Reps							
	Weight							
	Reps							
	Weight							
	Reps							
	Weight							
	Reps							
	Weight							

Cardio	Duration	Distance	Heart Rate	Calories

Measurements

Neck	R Bicep	Chest	Waist	Hips	R Thigh	L Thigh	Calf

Note	

Date			Start Time	
Muscle Group			Finish Time	
Weight			Upper Body	
Lower Body			Abs	

Exercise	Sets	Set 1	Set 2	Set 3	Set 4	Set 5	Set 6	Set 7
	Reps							
	Weight							
	Reps							
	Weight							
	Reps							
	Weight							
	Reps							
	Weight							
	Reps							
	Weight							
	Reps							
	Weight							
	Reps							
	Weight							
	Reps							
	Weight							
	Reps							
	Weight							

Cardio	Duration	Distance	Heart Rate	Calories

Measurements

Neck	R Bicep	Chest	Waist	Hips	R Thigh	L Thigh	Calf

Note	

Date				Start Time			
Muscle Group				Finish Time			
Weight				Upper Body			
Lower Body				Abs			

Exercise	Sets	Set 1	Set 2	Set 3	Set 4	Set 5	Set 6	Set 7
	Reps							
	Weight							
	Reps							
	Weight							
	Reps							
	Weight							
	Reps							
	Weight							
	Reps							
	Weight							
	Reps							
	Weight							
	Reps							
	Weight							
	Reps							
	Weight							
	Reps							
	Weight							

Cardio	Duration	Distance	Heart Rate	Calories

Measurements

Neck	R Bicep	Chest	Waist	Hips	R Thigh	L Thigh	Calf

Note	

Date		Start Time	
Muscle Group		Finish Time	
Weight		Upper Body	
Lower Body		Abs	

Exercise	Sets	Set 1	Set 2	Set 3	Set 4	Set 5	Set 6	Set 7
	Reps							
	Weight							
	Reps							
	Weight							
	Reps							
	Weight							
	Reps							
	Weight							
	Reps							
	Weight							
	Reps							
	Weight							
	Reps							
	Weight							
	Reps							
	Weight							
	Reps							
	Weight							

Cardio	Duration	Distance	Heart Rate	Calories

Measurements

Neck	R Bicep	Chest	Waist	Hips	R Thigh	L Thigh	Calf

Note	

Date				Start Time				
Muscle Group				Finish Time				
Weight				Upper Body				
Lower Body				Abs				

Exercise	Sets	Set 1	Set 2	Set 3	Set 4	Set 5	Set 6	Set 7
	Reps							
	Weight							
	Reps							
	Weight							
	Reps							
	Weight							
	Reps							
	Weight							
	Reps							
	Weight							
	Reps							
	Weight							
	Reps							
	Weight							
	Reps							
	Weight							
	Reps							
	Weight							

Cardio	Duration	Distance	Heart Rate	Calories

Measurements

Neck	R Bicep	Chest	Waist	Hips	R Thigh	L Thigh	Calf

Note

Date			Start Time		
Muscle Group			Finish Time		
Weight			Upper Body		
Lower Body			Abs		

Exercise	Sets	Set 1	Set 2	Set 3	Set 4	Set 5	Set 6	Set 7
	Reps							
	Weight							
	Reps							
	Weight							
	Reps							
	Weight							
	Reps							
	Weight							
	Reps							
	Weight							
	Reps							
	Weight							
	Reps							
	Weight							
	Reps							
	Weight							
	Reps							
	Weight							

Cardio	Duration	Distance	Heart Rate	Calories

Measurements

Neck	R Bicep	Chest	Waist	Hips	R Thigh	L Thigh	Calf

Note	

Date			Start Time	
Muscle Group			Finish Time	
Weight			Upper Body	
Lower Body			Abs	

Exercise	Sets	Set 1	Set 2	Set 3	Set 4	Set 5	Set 6	Set 7
	Reps							
	Weight							
	Reps							
	Weight							
	Reps							
	Weight							
	Reps							
	Weight							
	Reps							
	Weight							
	Reps							
	Weight							
	Reps							
	Weight							
	Reps							
	Weight							
	Reps							
	Weight							

Cardio	Duration	Distance	Heart Rate	Calories

Measurements

Neck	R Bicep	Chest	Waist	Hips	R Thigh	L Thigh	Calf

Note

Date		Start Time	
Muscle Group		Finish Time	
Weight		Upper Body	
Lower Body		Abs	

Exercise	Sets	Set 1	Set 2	Set 3	Set 4	Set 5	Set 6	Set 7
	Reps							
	Weight							
	Reps							
	Weight							
	Reps							
	Weight							
	Reps							
	Weight							
	Reps							
	Weight							
	Reps							
	Weight							
	Reps							
	Weight							
	Reps							
	Weight							
	Reps							
	Weight							

Cardio	Duration	Distance	Heart Rate	Calories

Measurements

Neck	R Bicep	Chest	Waist	Hips	R Thigh	L Thigh	Calf

Note

Date				Start Time				
Muscle Group				Finish Time				
Weight				Upper Body				
Lower Body				Abs				

Exercise	Sets	Set 1	Set 2	Set 3	Set 4	Set 5	Set 6	Set 7
	Reps							
	Weight							
	Reps							
	Weight							
	Reps							
	Weight							
	Reps							
	Weight							
	Reps							
	Weight							
	Reps							
	Weight							
	Reps							
	Weight							
	Reps							
	Weight							
	Reps							
	Weight							

Cardio	Duration	Distance	Heart Rate	Calories

Measurements

Neck	R Bicep	Chest	Waist	Hips	R Thigh	L Thigh	Calf

Note

Date				Start Time			
Muscle Group				Finish Time			
Weight				Upper Body			
Lower Body				Abs			

Exercise	Sets	Set 1	Set 2	Set 3	Set 4	Set 5	Set 6	Set 7
	Reps							
	Weight							
	Reps							
	Weight							
	Reps							
	Weight							
	Reps							
	Weight							
	Reps							
	Weight							
	Reps							
	Weight							
	Reps							
	Weight							
	Reps							
	Weight							
	Reps							
	Weight							

Cardio	Duration	Distance	Heart Rate	Calories

Measurements

Neck	R Bicep	Chest	Waist	Hips	R Thigh	L Thigh	Calf

Note	

Date				Start Time				
Muscle Group				Finish Time				
Weight				Upper Body				
Lower Body				Abs				

Exercise	Sets	Set 1	Set 2	Set 3	Set 4	Set 5	Set 6	Set 7
	Reps							
	Weight							
	Reps							
	Weight							
	Reps							
	Weight							
	Reps							
	Weight							
	Reps							
	Weight							
	Reps							
	Weight							
	Reps							
	Weight							
	Reps							
	Weight							
	Reps							
	Weight							

Cardio	Duration	Distance	Heart Rate	Calories

Measurements

Neck	R Bicep	Chest	Waist	Hips	R Thigh	L Thigh	Calf

Note

Date		Start Time	
Muscle Group		Finish Time	
Weight		Upper Body	
Lower Body		Abs	

Exercise	Sets	Set 1	Set 2	Set 3	Set 4	Set 5	Set 6	Set 7
	Reps							
	Weight							
	Reps							
	Weight							
	Reps							
	Weight							
	Reps							
	Weight							
	Reps							
	Weight							
	Reps							
	Weight							
	Reps							
	Weight							
	Reps							
	Weight							
	Reps							
	Weight							

Cardio	Duration	Distance	Heart Rate	Calories

Measurements

Neck	R Bicep	Chest	Waist	Hips	R Thigh	L Thigh	Calf

Note	

Date				Start Time				
Muscle Group				Finish Time				
Weight				Upper Body				
Lower Body				Abs				

Exercise	Sets	Set 1	Set 2	Set 3	Set 4	Set 5	Set 6	Set 7
	Reps							
	Weight							
	Reps							
	Weight							
	Reps							
	Weight							
	Reps							
	Weight							
	Reps							
	Weight							
	Reps							
	Weight							
	Reps							
	Weight							
	Reps							
	Weight							
	Reps							
	Weight							

Cardio	Duration	Distance	Heart Rate	Calories

Measurements

Neck	R Bicep	Chest	Waist	Hips	R Thigh	L Thigh	Calf

Note

Date		Start Time	
Muscle Group		Finish Time	
Weight		Upper Body	
Lower Body		Abs	

Exercise	Sets	Set 1	Set 2	Set 3	Set 4	Set 5	Set 6	Set 7
	Reps							
	Weight							
	Reps							
	Weight							
	Reps							
	Weight							
	Reps							
	Weight							
	Reps							
	Weight							
	Reps							
	Weight							
	Reps							
	Weight							
	Reps							
	Weight							
	Reps							
	Weight							

Cardio	Duration	Distance	Heart Rate	Calories

Measurements

Neck	R Bicep	Chest	Waist	Hips	R Thigh	L Thigh	Calf

Note	

Date					Start Time			
Muscle Group					Finish Time			
Weight					Upper Body			
Lower Body					Abs			

Exercise	Sets	Set 1	Set 2	Set 3	Set 4	Set 5	Set 6	Set 7
	Reps							
	Weight							
	Reps							
	Weight							
	Reps							
	Weight							
	Reps							
	Weight							
	Reps							
	Weight							
	Reps							
	Weight							
	Reps							
	Weight							
	Reps							
	Weight							
	Reps							
	Weight							

Cardio	Duration	Distance	Heart Rate	Calories

Measurements

Neck	R Bicep	Chest	Waist	Hips	R Thigh	L Thigh	Calf

Note

Date				Start Time			
Muscle Group				Finish Time			
Weight				Upper Body			
Lower Body				Abs			

Exercise	Sets	Set 1	Set 2	Set 3	Set 4	Set 5	Set 6	Set 7
	Reps							
	Weight							
	Reps							
	Weight							
	Reps							
	Weight							
	Reps							
	Weight							
	Reps							
	Weight							
	Reps							
	Weight							
	Reps							
	Weight							
	Reps							
	Weight							
	Reps							
	Weight							

Cardio	Duration	Distance	Heart Rate	Calories

Measurements

Neck	R Bicep	Chest	Waist	Hips	R Thigh	L Thigh	Calf

Note	

Date				Start Time				

Muscle Group				Finish Time				

Weight				Upper Body				

Lower Body				Abs				

Exercise	Sets	Set 1	Set 2	Set 3	Set 4	Set 5	Set 6	Set 7
	Reps							
	Weight							
	Reps							
	Weight							
	Reps							
	Weight							
	Reps							
	Weight							
	Reps							
	Weight							
	Reps							
	Weight							
	Reps							
	Weight							
	Reps							
	Weight							
	Reps							
	Weight							

Cardio	Duration	Distance	Heart Rate	Calories

Measurements

Neck	R Bicep	Chest	Waist	Hips	R Thigh	L Thigh	Calf

Note	

Date				Start Time				
Muscle Group				Finish Time				
Weight				Upper Body				
Lower Body				Abs				

Exercise	Sets	Set 1	Set 2	Set 3	Set 4	Set 5	Set 6	Set 7
	Reps							
	Weight							
	Reps							
	Weight							
	Reps							
	Weight							
	Reps							
	Weight							
	Reps							
	Weight							
	Reps							
	Weight							
	Reps							
	Weight							
	Reps							
	Weight							
	Reps							
	Weight							

Cardio	Duration	Distance	Heart Rate	Calories

Measurements

Neck	R Bicep	Chest	Waist	Hips	R Thigh	L Thigh	Calf

Note	

Date		Start Time	
Muscle Group		Finish Time	
Weight		Upper Body	
Lower Body		Abs	

Exercise	Sets	Set 1	Set 2	Set 3	Set 4	Set 5	Set 6	Set 7
	Reps							
	Weight							
	Reps							
	Weight							
	Reps							
	Weight							
	Reps							
	Weight							
	Reps							
	Weight							
	Reps							
	Weight							
	Reps							
	Weight							
	Reps							
	Weight							
	Reps							
	Weight							

Cardio	Duration	Distance	Heart Rate	Calories

Measurements

Neck	R Bicep	Chest	Waist	Hips	R Thigh	L Thigh	Calf

Note

Date			Start Time	
Muscle Group			Finish Time	
Weight			Upper Body	
Lower Body			Abs	

Exercise	Sets	Set 1	Set 2	Set 3	Set 4	Set 5	Set 6	Set 7
	Reps							
	Weight							
	Reps							
	Weight							
	Reps							
	Weight							
	Reps							
	Weight							
	Reps							
	Weight							
	Reps							
	Weight							
	Reps							
	Weight							
	Reps							
	Weight							
	Reps							
	Weight							

Cardio	Duration	Distance	Heart Rate	Calories

Measurements

Neck	R Bicep	Chest	Waist	Hips	R Thigh	L Thigh	Calf

Note

Date				Start Time			
Muscle Group				Finish Time			
Weight				Upper Body			
Lower Body				Abs			

Exercise	Sets	Set 1	Set 2	Set 3	Set 4	Set 5	Set 6	Set 7
	Reps							
	Weight							
	Reps							
	Weight							
	Reps							
	Weight							
	Reps							
	Weight							
	Reps							
	Weight							
	Reps							
	Weight							
	Reps							
	Weight							
	Reps							
	Weight							
	Reps							
	Weight							

Cardio	Duration	Distance	Heart Rate	Calories

Measurements

Neck	R Bicep	Chest	Waist	Hips	R Thigh	L Thigh	Calf

Note

Date			Start Time	
Muscle Group			Finish Time	
Weight			Upper Body	
Lower Body			Abs	

Exercise	Sets	Set 1	Set 2	Set 3	Set 4	Set 5	Set 6	Set 7
	Reps							
	Weight							
	Reps							
	Weight							
	Reps							
	Weight							
	Reps							
	Weight							
	Reps							
	Weight							
	Reps							
	Weight							
	Reps							
	Weight							
	Reps							
	Weight							
	Reps							
	Weight							

Cardio	Duration	Distance	Heart Rate	Calories

Measurements

Neck	R Bicep	Chest	Waist	Hips	R Thigh	L Thigh	Calf

Note	

Date				Start Time				

Muscle Group				Finish Time				

Weight				Upper Body				

Lower Body				Abs				

Exercise	Sets	Set 1	Set 2	Set 3	Set 4	Set 5	Set 6	Set 7
	Reps							
	Weight							
	Reps							
	Weight							
	Reps							
	Weight							
	Reps							
	Weight							
	Reps							
	Weight							
	Reps							
	Weight							
	Reps							
	Weight							
	Reps							
	Weight							
	Reps							
	Weight							

Cardio	Duration	Distance	Heart Rate	Calories

Measurements

Neck	R Bicep	Chest	Waist	Hips	R Thigh	L Thigh	Calf

Note	

Date			Start Time		
Muscle Group			Finish Time		
Weight			Upper Body		
Lower Body			Abs		

Exercise	Sets	Set 1	Set 2	Set 3	Set 4	Set 5	Set 6	Set 7
	Reps							
	Weight							
	Reps							
	Weight							
	Reps							
	Weight							
	Reps							
	Weight							
	Reps							
	Weight							
	Reps							
	Weight							
	Reps							
	Weight							
	Reps							
	Weight							
	Reps							
	Weight							

Cardio	Duration	Distance	Heart Rate	Calories

Measurements

Neck	R Bicep	Chest	Waist	Hips	R Thigh	L Thigh	Calf

Note	

Date					Start Time			
Muscle Group					Finish Time			
Weight					Upper Body			
Lower Body					Abs			

Exercise	Sets	Set 1	Set 2	Set 3	Set 4	Set 5	Set 6	Set 7
	Reps							
	Weight							
	Reps							
	Weight							
	Reps							
	Weight							
	Reps							
	Weight							
	Reps							
	Weight							
	Reps							
	Weight							
	Reps							
	Weight							
	Reps							
	Weight							
	Reps							
	Weight							

Cardio	Duration	Distance	Heart Rate	Calories

Measurements							
Neck	R Bicep	Chest	Waist	Hips	R Thigh	L Thigh	Calf

Note	

Date			Start Time	
Muscle Group			Finish Time	
Weight			Upper Body	
Lower Body			Abs	

Exercise	Sets	Set 1	Set 2	Set 3	Set 4	Set 5	Set 6	Set 7
	Reps							
	Weight							
	Reps							
	Weight							
	Reps							
	Weight							
	Reps							
	Weight							
	Reps							
	Weight							
	Reps							
	Weight							
	Reps							
	Weight							
	Reps							
	Weight							
	Reps							
	Weight							

Cardio	Duration	Distance	Heart Rate	Calories

Measurements

Neck	R Bicep	Chest	Waist	Hips	R Thigh	L Thigh	Calf

Note	

Date		Start Time	
Muscle Group		Finish Time	
Weight		Upper Body	
Lower Body		Abs	

Exercise	Sets	Set 1	Set 2	Set 3	Set 4	Set 5	Set 6	Set 7
	Reps							
	Weight							
	Reps							
	Weight							
	Reps							
	Weight							
	Reps							
	Weight							
	Reps							
	Weight							
	Reps							
	Weight							
	Reps							
	Weight							
	Reps							
	Weight							
	Reps							
	Weight							

Cardio	Duration	Distance	Heart Rate	Calories

Measurements

Neck	R Bicep	Chest	Waist	Hips	R Thigh	L Thigh	Calf

Note

Date			Start Time		
Muscle Group			Finish Time		
Weight			Upper Body		
Lower Body			Abs		

Exercise	Sets	Set 1	Set 2	Set 3	Set 4	Set 5	Set 6	Set 7
	Reps							
	Weight							
	Reps							
	Weight							
	Reps							
	Weight							
	Reps							
	Weight							
	Reps							
	Weight							
	Reps							
	Weight							
	Reps							
	Weight							
	Reps							
	Weight							
	Reps							
	Weight							

Cardio	Duration	Distance	Heart Rate	Calories

Measurements

Neck	R Bicep	Chest	Waist	Hips	R Thigh	L Thigh	Calf

Note	

Date				Start Time				
Muscle Group				Finish Time				
Weight				Upper Body				
Lower Body				Abs				

Exercise	Sets	Set 1	Set 2	Set 3	Set 4	Set 5	Set 6	Set 7
	Reps							
	Weight							
	Reps							
	Weight							
	Reps							
	Weight							
	Reps							
	Weight							
	Reps							
	Weight							
	Reps							
	Weight							
	Reps							
	Weight							
	Reps							
	Weight							
	Reps							
	Weight							

Cardio	Duration	Distance	Heart Rate	Calories

Measurements

Neck	R Bicep	Chest	Waist	Hips	R Thigh	L Thigh	Calf

Note	

Date				Start Time				
Muscle Group				Finish Time				
Weight				Upper Body				
Lower Body				Abs				

Exercise	Sets	Set 1	Set 2	Set 3	Set 4	Set 5	Set 6	Set 7
	Reps							
	Weight							
	Reps							
	Weight							
	Reps							
	Weight							
	Reps							
	Weight							
	Reps							
	Weight							
	Reps							
	Weight							
	Reps							
	Weight							
	Reps							
	Weight							
	Reps							
	Weight							

Cardio	Duration	Distance	Heart Rate	Calories

Measurements

Neck	R Bicep	Chest	Waist	Hips	R Thigh	L Thigh	Calf

Note	

Date				Start Time				
Muscle Group				Finish Time				
Weight				Upper Body				
Lower Body				Abs				

Exercise	Sets	Set 1	Set 2	Set 3	Set 4	Set 5	Set 6	Set 7
	Reps							
	Weight							
	Reps							
	Weight							
	Reps							
	Weight							
	Reps							
	Weight							
	Reps							
	Weight							
	Reps							
	Weight							
	Reps							
	Weight							
	Reps							
	Weight							
	Reps							
	Weight							

Cardio	Duration	Distance	Heart Rate	Calories

Measurements

Neck	R Bicep	Chest	Waist	Hips	R Thigh	L Thigh	Calf

Note

Date				Start Time			
Muscle Group				Finish Time			
Weight				Upper Body			
Lower Body				Abs			

Exercise	Sets	Set 1	Set 2	Set 3	Set 4	Set 5	Set 6	Set 7
	Reps							
	Weight							
	Reps							
	Weight							
	Reps							
	Weight							
	Reps							
	Weight							
	Reps							
	Weight							
	Reps							
	Weight							
	Reps							
	Weight							
	Reps							
	Weight							
	Reps							
	Weight							

Cardio	Duration	Distance	Heart Rate	Calories

Measurements

Neck	R Bicep	Chest	Waist	Hips	R Thigh	L Thigh	Calf

Note	

Date				Start Time				
Muscle Group				Finish Time				
Weight				Upper Body				
Lower Body				Abs				

Exercise	Sets	Set 1	Set 2	Set 3	Set 4	Set 5	Set 6	Set 7
	Reps							
	Weight							
	Reps							
	Weight							
	Reps							
	Weight							
	Reps							
	Weight							
	Reps							
	Weight							
	Reps							
	Weight							
	Reps							
	Weight							
	Reps							
	Weight							
	Reps							
	Weight							

Cardio	Duration	Distance	Heart Rate	Calories

Measurements

Neck	R Bicep	Chest	Waist	Hips	R Thigh	L Thigh	Calf

Note	

Date			Start Time	
Muscle Group			Finish Time	
Weight			Upper Body	
Lower Body			Abs	

Exercise	Sets	Set 1	Set 2	Set 3	Set 4	Set 5	Set 6	Set 7
	Reps							
	Weight							
	Reps							
	Weight							
	Reps							
	Weight							
	Reps							
	Weight							
	Reps							
	Weight							
	Reps							
	Weight							
	Reps							
	Weight							
	Reps							
	Weight							
	Reps							
	Weight							

Cardio	Duration	Distance	Heart Rate	Calories

Measurements

Neck	R Bicep	Chest	Waist	Hips	R Thigh	L Thigh	Calf

Note	

Date				Start Time				

Muscle Group				Finish Time				

Weight				Upper Body				

Lower Body				Abs				

Exercise	Sets	Set 1	Set 2	Set 3	Set 4	Set 5	Set 6	Set 7
	Reps							
	Weight							
	Reps							
	Weight							
	Reps							
	Weight							
	Reps							
	Weight							
	Reps							
	Weight							
	Reps							
	Weight							
	Reps							
	Weight							
	Reps							
	Weight							
	Reps							
	Weight							

Cardio	Duration	Distance	Heart Rate	Calories

Measurements

Neck	R Bicep	Chest	Waist	Hips	R Thigh	L Thigh	Calf

Note	

Date					Start Time			
Muscle Group					Finish Time			
Weight					Upper Body			
Lower Body					Abs			

Exercise	Sets	Set 1	Set 2	Set 3	Set 4	Set 5	Set 6	Set 7
	Reps							
	Weight							
	Reps							
	Weight							
	Reps							
	Weight							
	Reps							
	Weight							
	Reps							
	Weight							
	Reps							
	Weight							
	Reps							
	Weight							
	Reps							
	Weight							
	Reps							
	Weight							

Cardio	Duration	Distance	Heart Rate	Calories

Measurements

Neck	R Bicep	Chest	Waist	Hips	R Thigh	L Thigh	Calf

Note	

Date				Start Time				
Muscle Group				Finish Time				
Weight				Upper Body				
Lower Body				Abs				

Exercise	Sets	Set 1	Set 2	Set 3	Set 4	Set 5	Set 6	Set 7
	Reps							
	Weight							
	Reps							
	Weight							
	Reps							
	Weight							
	Reps							
	Weight							
	Reps							
	Weight							
	Reps							
	Weight							
	Reps							
	Weight							
	Reps							
	Weight							
	Reps							
	Weight							

Cardio	Duration	Distance	Heart Rate	Calories

Measurements

Neck	R Bicep	Chest	Waist	Hips	R Thigh	L Thigh	Calf

Note

Date				Start Time				
Muscle Group				Finish Time				
Weight				Upper Body				
Lower Body				Abs				

Exercise	Sets	Set 1	Set 2	Set 3	Set 4	Set 5	Set 6	Set 7
	Reps							
	Weight							
	Reps							
	Weight							
	Reps							
	Weight							
	Reps							
	Weight							
	Reps							
	Weight							
	Reps							
	Weight							
	Reps							
	Weight							
	Reps							
	Weight							
	Reps							
	Weight							

Cardio	Duration	Distance	Heart Rate	Calories

Measurements

Neck	R Bicep	Chest	Waist	Hips	R Thigh	L Thigh	Calf

Note	

Date				Start Time			
Muscle Group				Finish Time			
Weight				Upper Body			
Lower Body				Abs			

Exercise	Sets	Set 1	Set 2	Set 3	Set 4	Set 5	Set 6	Set 7
	Reps							
	Weight							
	Reps							
	Weight							
	Reps							
	Weight							
	Reps							
	Weight							
	Reps							
	Weight							
	Reps							
	Weight							
	Reps							
	Weight							
	Reps							
	Weight							
	Reps							
	Weight							

Cardio	Duration	Distance	Heart Rate	Calories

Measurements

Neck	R Bicep	Chest	Waist	Hips	R Thigh	L Thigh	Calf

Note	

Date				Start Time				
Muscle Group				Finish Time				
Weight				Upper Body				
Lower Body				Abs				

Exercise	Sets	Set 1	Set 2	Set 3	Set 4	Set 5	Set 6	Set 7
	Reps							
	Weight							
	Reps							
	Weight							
	Reps							
	Weight							
	Reps							
	Weight							
	Reps							
	Weight							
	Reps							
	Weight							
	Reps							
	Weight							
	Reps							
	Weight							
	Reps							
	Weight							

Cardio	Duration	Distance	Heart Rate	Calories

Measurements

Neck	R Bicep	Chest	Waist	Hips	R Thigh	L Thigh	Calf

Note	

Date				Start Time				
Muscle Group				Finish Time				
Weight				Upper Body				
Lower Body				Abs				

Exercise	Sets	Set 1	Set 2	Set 3	Set 4	Set 5	Set 6	Set 7
	Reps							
	Weight							
	Reps							
	Weight							
	Reps							
	Weight							
	Reps							
	Weight							
	Reps							
	Weight							
	Reps							
	Weight							
	Reps							
	Weight							
	Reps							
	Weight							
	Reps							
	Weight							

Cardio	Duration	Distance	Heart Rate	Calories

Measurements

Neck	R Bicep	Chest	Waist	Hips	R Thigh	L Thigh	Calf

Note	

Date				Start Time				
Muscle Group				Finish Time				
Weight				Upper Body				
Lower Body				Abs				

Exercise	Sets	Set 1	Set 2	Set 3	Set 4	Set 5	Set 6	Set 7
	Reps							
	Weight							
	Reps							
	Weight							
	Reps							
	Weight							
	Reps							
	Weight							
	Reps							
	Weight							
	Reps							
	Weight							
	Reps							
	Weight							
	Reps							
	Weight							
	Reps							
	Weight							

Cardio	Duration	Distance	Heart Rate	Calories

Measurements

Neck	R Bicep	Chest	Waist	Hips	R Thigh	L Thigh	Calf

Note	

Date				Start Time				
Muscle Group				Finish Time				
Weight				Upper Body				
Lower Body				Abs				

Exercise	Sets	Set 1	Set 2	Set 3	Set 4	Set 5	Set 6	Set 7
	Reps							
	Weight							
	Reps							
	Weight							
	Reps							
	Weight							
	Reps							
	Weight							
	Reps							
	Weight							
	Reps							
	Weight							
	Reps							
	Weight							
	Reps							
	Weight							
	Reps							
	Weight							

Cardio	Duration	Distance	Heart Rate	Calories

Measurements

Neck	R Bicep	Chest	Waist	Hips	R Thigh	L Thigh	Calf

Note

Date				Start Time			
Muscle Group				Finish Time			
Weight				Upper Body			
Lower Body				Abs			

Exercise	Sets	Set 1	Set 2	Set 3	Set 4	Set 5	Set 6	Set 7
	Reps							
	Weight							
	Reps							
	Weight							
	Reps							
	Weight							
	Reps							
	Weight							
	Reps							
	Weight							
	Reps							
	Weight							
	Reps							
	Weight							
	Reps							
	Weight							
	Reps							
	Weight							

Cardio	Duration	Distance	Heart Rate	Calories

Measurements

Neck	R Bicep	Chest	Waist	Hips	R Thigh	L Thigh	Calf

Note	

Date					Start Time			
Muscle Group					Finish Time			
Weight					Upper Body			
Lower Body					Abs			

Exercise	Sets	Set 1	Set 2	Set 3	Set 4	Set 5	Set 6	Set 7
	Reps							
	Weight							
	Reps							
	Weight							
	Reps							
	Weight							
	Reps							
	Weight							
	Reps							
	Weight							
	Reps							
	Weight							
	Reps							
	Weight							
	Reps							
	Weight							
	Reps							
	Weight							

Cardio	Duration	Distance	Heart Rate	Calories

Measurements

Neck	R Bicep	Chest	Waist	Hips	R Thigh	L Thigh	Calf

Note

Date			Start Time	
Muscle Group			Finish Time	
Weight			Upper Body	
Lower Body			Abs	

Exercise	Sets	Set 1	Set 2	Set 3	Set 4	Set 5	Set 6	Set 7
	Reps							
	Weight							
	Reps							
	Weight							
	Reps							
	Weight							
	Reps							
	Weight							
	Reps							
	Weight							
	Reps							
	Weight							
	Reps							
	Weight							
	Reps							
	Weight							
	Reps							
	Weight							

Cardio	Duration	Distance	Heart Rate	Calories

Measurements

Neck	R Bicep	Chest	Waist	Hips	R Thigh	L Thigh	Calf

Note	

Date				Start Time				

Muscle Group				Finish Time				

Weight				Upper Body				

Lower Body				Abs				

Exercise	Sets	Set 1	Set 2	Set 3	Set 4	Set 5	Set 6	Set 7
	Reps							
	Weight							
	Reps							
	Weight							
	Reps							
	Weight							
	Reps							
	Weight							
	Reps							
	Weight							
	Reps							
	Weight							
	Reps							
	Weight							
	Reps							
	Weight							
	Reps							
	Weight							

Cardio	Duration	Distance	Heart Rate	Calories

Measurements							
Neck	R Bicep	Chest	Waist	Hips	R Thigh	L Thigh	Calf

Note	

Date		Start Time	
Muscle Group		Finish Time	
Weight		Upper Body	
Lower Body		Abs	

Exercise	Sets	Set 1	Set 2	Set 3	Set 4	Set 5	Set 6	Set 7
	Reps							
	Weight							
	Reps							
	Weight							
	Reps							
	Weight							
	Reps							
	Weight							
	Reps							
	Weight							
	Reps							
	Weight							
	Reps							
	Weight							
	Reps							
	Weight							
	Reps							
	Weight							

Cardio	Duration	Distance	Heart Rate	Calories

Measurements

Neck	R Bicep	Chest	Waist	Hips	R Thigh	L Thigh	Calf

Note	

Date				Start Time				
Muscle Group				Finish Time				
Weight				Upper Body				
Lower Body				Abs				

Exercise	Sets	Set 1	Set 2	Set 3	Set 4	Set 5	Set 6	Set 7
	Reps							
	Weight							
	Reps							
	Weight							
	Reps							
	Weight							
	Reps							
	Weight							
	Reps							
	Weight							
	Reps							
	Weight							
	Reps							
	Weight							
	Reps							
	Weight							
	Reps							
	Weight							

Cardio	Duration	Distance	Heart Rate	Calories

Measurements

Neck	R Bicep	Chest	Waist	Hips	R Thigh	L Thigh	Calf

Note

Date				Start Time			
Muscle Group				Finish Time			
Weight				Upper Body			
Lower Body				Abs			

Exercise	Sets	Set 1	Set 2	Set 3	Set 4	Set 5	Set 6	Set 7
	Reps							
	Weight							
	Reps							
	Weight							
	Reps							
	Weight							
	Reps							
	Weight							
	Reps							
	Weight							
	Reps							
	Weight							
	Reps							
	Weight							
	Reps							
	Weight							
	Reps							
	Weight							

Cardio	Duration	Distance	Heart Rate	Calories

Measurements

Neck	R Bicep	Chest	Waist	Hips	R Thigh	L Thigh	Calf

Note

Date				Start Time			
Muscle Group				Finish Time			
Weight				Upper Body			
Lower Body				Abs			

Exercise	Sets	Set 1	Set 2	Set 3	Set 4	Set 5	Set 6	Set 7
	Reps							
	Weight							
	Reps							
	Weight							
	Reps							
	Weight							
	Reps							
	Weight							
	Reps							
	Weight							
	Reps							
	Weight							
	Reps							
	Weight							
	Reps							
	Weight							
	Reps							
	Weight							

Cardio	Duration	Distance	Heart Rate	Calories

Measurements

Neck	R Bicep	Chest	Waist	Hips	R Thigh	L Thigh	Calf

Note	

Date				Start Time			
Muscle Group				Finish Time			
Weight				Upper Body			
Lower Body				Abs			

Exercise	Sets	Set 1	Set 2	Set 3	Set 4	Set 5	Set 6	Set 7
	Reps							
	Weight							
	Reps							
	Weight							
	Reps							
	Weight							
	Reps							
	Weight							
	Reps							
	Weight							
	Reps							
	Weight							
	Reps							
	Weight							
	Reps							
	Weight							
	Reps							
	Weight							

Cardio	Duration	Distance	Heart Rate	Calories

Measurements

Neck	R Bicep	Chest	Waist	Hips	R Thigh	L Thigh	Calf

Note	

Date				Start Time			
Muscle Group				Finish Time			
Weight				Upper Body			
Lower Body				Abs			

Exercise	Sets	Set 1	Set 2	Set 3	Set 4	Set 5	Set 6	Set 7
	Reps							
	Weight							
	Reps							
	Weight							
	Reps							
	Weight							
	Reps							
	Weight							
	Reps							
	Weight							
	Reps							
	Weight							
	Reps							
	Weight							
	Reps							
	Weight							
	Reps							
	Weight							

Cardio	Duration	Distance	Heart Rate	Calories

Measurements

Neck	R Bicep	Chest	Waist	Hips	R Thigh	L Thigh	Calf

Note

Date		Start Time	
Muscle Group		Finish Time	
Weight		Upper Body	
Lower Body		Abs	

Exercise	Sets	Set 1	Set 2	Set 3	Set 4	Set 5	Set 6	Set 7
	Reps							
	Weight							
	Reps							
	Weight							
	Reps							
	Weight							
	Reps							
	Weight							
	Reps							
	Weight							
	Reps							
	Weight							
	Reps							
	Weight							
	Reps							
	Weight							
	Reps							
	Weight							

Cardio	Duration	Distance	Heart Rate	Calories

Measurements

Neck	R Bicep	Chest	Waist	Hips	R Thigh	L Thigh	Calf

Note	

Date				Start Time			
Muscle Group				Finish Time			
Weight				Upper Body			
Lower Body				Abs			

Exercise	Sets	Set 1	Set 2	Set 3	Set 4	Set 5	Set 6	Set 7
	Reps							
	Weight							
	Reps							
	Weight							
	Reps							
	Weight							
	Reps							
	Weight							
	Reps							
	Weight							
	Reps							
	Weight							
	Reps							
	Weight							
	Reps							
	Weight							
	Reps							
	Weight							

Cardio	Duration	Distance	Heart Rate	Calories

Measurements

Neck	R Bicep	Chest	Waist	Hips	R Thigh	L Thigh	Calf

Note

Date			Start Time	
Muscle Group			Finish Time	
Weight			Upper Body	
Lower Body			Abs	

Exercise	Sets	Set 1	Set 2	Set 3	Set 4	Set 5	Set 6	Set 7
	Reps							
	Weight							
	Reps							
	Weight							
	Reps							
	Weight							
	Reps							
	Weight							
	Reps							
	Weight							
	Reps							
	Weight							
	Reps							
	Weight							
	Reps							
	Weight							
	Reps							
	Weight							

Cardio	Duration	Distance	Heart Rate	Calories

Measurements

Neck	R Bicep	Chest	Waist	Hips	R Thigh	L Thigh	Calf

Note

Date				Start Time			
Muscle Group				Finish Time			
Weight				Upper Body			
Lower Body				Abs			

Exercise	Sets	Set 1	Set 2	Set 3	Set 4	Set 5	Set 6	Set 7
	Reps							
	Weight							
	Reps							
	Weight							
	Reps							
	Weight							
	Reps							
	Weight							
	Reps							
	Weight							
	Reps							
	Weight							
	Reps							
	Weight							
	Reps							
	Weight							
	Reps							
	Weight							

Cardio	Duration	Distance	Heart Rate	Calories

Measurements

Neck	R Bicep	Chest	Waist	Hips	R Thigh	L Thigh	Calf

Note

Date			Start Time				
Muscle Group			Finish Time				
Weight			Upper Body				
Lower Body			Abs				

Exercise	Sets	Set 1	Set 2	Set 3	Set 4	Set 5	Set 6	Set 7
	Reps							
	Weight							
	Reps							
	Weight							
	Reps							
	Weight							
	Reps							
	Weight							
	Reps							
	Weight							
	Reps							
	Weight							
	Reps							
	Weight							
	Reps							
	Weight							
	Reps							
	Weight							

Cardio	Duration	Distance	Heart Rate	Calories

Measurements

Neck	R Bicep	Chest	Waist	Hips	R Thigh	L Thigh	Calf

Note	

Date				Start Time				
Muscle Group				Finish Time				
Weight				Upper Body				
Lower Body				Abs				

Exercise	Sets	Set 1	Set 2	Set 3	Set 4	Set 5	Set 6	Set 7
	Reps							
	Weight							
	Reps							
	Weight							
	Reps							
	Weight							
	Reps							
	Weight							
	Reps							
	Weight							
	Reps							
	Weight							
	Reps							
	Weight							
	Reps							
	Weight							
	Reps							
	Weight							

Cardio	Duration	Distance	Heart Rate	Calories

Measurements

Neck	R Bicep	Chest	Waist	Hips	R Thigh	L Thigh	Calf

Note	

Date		Start Time	
Muscle Group		Finish Time	
Weight		Upper Body	
Lower Body		Abs	

Exercise	Sets	Set 1	Set 2	Set 3	Set 4	Set 5	Set 6	Set 7
	Reps							
	Weight							
	Reps							
	Weight							
	Reps							
	Weight							
	Reps							
	Weight							
	Reps							
	Weight							
	Reps							
	Weight							
	Reps							
	Weight							
	Reps							
	Weight							
	Reps							
	Weight							

Cardio	Duration	Distance	Heart Rate	Calories

Measurements

Neck	R Bicep	Chest	Waist	Hips	R Thigh	L Thigh	Calf

Note	

Date				Start Time			
Muscle Group				Finish Time			
Weight				Upper Body			
Lower Body				Abs			

Exercise	Sets	Set 1	Set 2	Set 3	Set 4	Set 5	Set 6	Set 7
	Reps							
	Weight							
	Reps							
	Weight							
	Reps							
	Weight							
	Reps							
	Weight							
	Reps							
	Weight							
	Reps							
	Weight							
	Reps							
	Weight							
	Reps							
	Weight							
	Reps							
	Weight							

Cardio	Duration	Distance	Heart Rate	Calories

Measurements

Neck	R Bicep	Chest	Waist	Hips	R Thigh	L Thigh	Calf

Note	

Date				Start Time			
Muscle Group				Finish Time			
Weight				Upper Body			
Lower Body				Abs			

Exercise	Sets	Set 1	Set 2	Set 3	Set 4	Set 5	Set 6	Set 7
	Reps							
	Weight							
	Reps							
	Weight							
	Reps							
	Weight							
	Reps							
	Weight							
	Reps							
	Weight							
	Reps							
	Weight							
	Reps							
	Weight							
	Reps							
	Weight							
	Reps							
	Weight							

Cardio	Duration	Distance	Heart Rate	Calories

Measurements

Neck	R Bicep	Chest	Waist	Hips	R Thigh	L Thigh	Calf

Note

Date				Start Time				
Muscle Group				Finish Time				
Weight				Upper Body				
Lower Body				Abs				

Exercise	Sets	Set 1	Set 2	Set 3	Set 4	Set 5	Set 6	Set 7
	Reps							
	Weight							
	Reps							
	Weight							
	Reps							
	Weight							
	Reps							
	Weight							
	Reps							
	Weight							
	Reps							
	Weight							
	Reps							
	Weight							
	Reps							
	Weight							
	Reps							
	Weight							

Cardio	Duration	Distance	Heart Rate	Calories

Measurements

Neck	R Bicep	Chest	Waist	Hips	R Thigh	L Thigh	Calf

Note	

Date		Start Time	
Muscle Group		Finish Time	
Weight		Upper Body	
Lower Body		Abs	

Exercise	Sets	Set 1	Set 2	Set 3	Set 4	Set 5	Set 6	Set 7
	Reps							
	Weight							
	Reps							
	Weight							
	Reps							
	Weight							
	Reps							
	Weight							
	Reps							
	Weight							
	Reps							
	Weight							
	Reps							
	Weight							
	Reps							
	Weight							
	Reps							
	Weight							

Cardio	Duration	Distance	Heart Rate	Calories

Measurements

Neck	R Bicep	Chest	Waist	Hips	R Thigh	L Thigh	Calf

Note	

Date				Start Time				
Muscle Group				Finish Time				
Weight				Upper Body				
Lower Body				Abs				

Exercise	Sets	Set 1	Set 2	Set 3	Set 4	Set 5	Set 6	Set 7
	Reps							
	Weight							
	Reps							
	Weight							
	Reps							
	Weight							
	Reps							
	Weight							
	Reps							
	Weight							
	Reps							
	Weight							
	Reps							
	Weight							
	Reps							
	Weight							
	Reps							
	Weight							

Cardio	Duration	Distance	Heart Rate	Calories

Measurements

Neck	R Bicep	Chest	Waist	Hips	R Thigh	L Thigh	Calf

Note	

Date			Start Time	
Muscle Group			Finish Time	
Weight			Upper Body	
Lower Body			Abs	

Exercise	Sets	Set 1	Set 2	Set 3	Set 4	Set 5	Set 6	Set 7
	Reps							
	Weight							
	Reps							
	Weight							
	Reps							
	Weight							
	Reps							
	Weight							
	Reps							
	Weight							
	Reps							
	Weight							
	Reps							
	Weight							
	Reps							
	Weight							
	Reps							
	Weight							

Cardio	Duration	Distance	Heart Rate	Calories

Measurements

Neck	R Bicep	Chest	Waist	Hips	R Thigh	L Thigh	Calf

Note	

Date		Start Time	
Muscle Group		Finish Time	
Weight		Upper Body	
Lower Body		Abs	

Exercise	Sets	Set 1	Set 2	Set 3	Set 4	Set 5	Set 6	Set 7
	Reps							
	Weight							
	Reps							
	Weight							
	Reps							
	Weight							
	Reps							
	Weight							
	Reps							
	Weight							
	Reps							
	Weight							
	Reps							
	Weight							
	Reps							
	Weight							
	Reps							
	Weight							

Cardio	Duration	Distance	Heart Rate	Calories

Measurements

Neck	R Bicep	Chest	Waist	Hips	R Thigh	L Thigh	Calf

Note	

Date			Start Time	
Muscle Group			Finish Time	
Weight			Upper Body	
Lower Body			Abs	

Exercise	Sets	Set 1	Set 2	Set 3	Set 4	Set 5	Set 6	Set 7
	Reps							
	Weight							
	Reps							
	Weight							
	Reps							
	Weight							
	Reps							
	Weight							
	Reps							
	Weight							
	Reps							
	Weight							
	Reps							
	Weight							
	Reps							
	Weight							
	Reps							
	Weight							

Cardio	Duration	Distance	Heart Rate	Calories

Measurements

Neck	R Bicep	Chest	Waist	Hips	R Thigh	L Thigh	Calf

Note

Date				Start Time				
Muscle Group				Finish Time				
Weight				Upper Body				
Lower Body				Abs				

Exercise	Sets	Set 1	Set 2	Set 3	Set 4	Set 5	Set 6	Set 7
	Reps							
	Weight							
	Reps							
	Weight							
	Reps							
	Weight							
	Reps							
	Weight							
	Reps							
	Weight							
	Reps							
	Weight							
	Reps							
	Weight							
	Reps							
	Weight							
	Reps							
	Weight							

Cardio	Duration	Distance	Heart Rate	Calories

Measurements

Neck	R Bicep	Chest	Waist	Hips	R Thigh	L Thigh	Calf

Note	

Date			Start Time	
Muscle Group			Finish Time	
Weight			Upper Body	
Lower Body			Abs	

Exercise	Sets	Set 1	Set 2	Set 3	Set 4	Set 5	Set 6	Set 7
	Reps							
	Weight							
	Reps							
	Weight							
	Reps							
	Weight							
	Reps							
	Weight							
	Reps							
	Weight							
	Reps							
	Weight							
	Reps							
	Weight							
	Reps							
	Weight							
	Reps							
	Weight							

Cardio	Duration	Distance	Heart Rate	Calories

Measurements

Neck	R Bicep	Chest	Waist	Hips	R Thigh	L Thigh	Calf

Note	

Date				Start Time				
Muscle Group				Finish Time				
Weight				Upper Body				
Lower Body				Abs				

Exercise	Sets	Set 1	Set 2	Set 3	Set 4	Set 5	Set 6	Set 7
	Reps							
	Weight							
	Reps							
	Weight							
	Reps							
	Weight							
	Reps							
	Weight							
	Reps							
	Weight							
	Reps							
	Weight							
	Reps							
	Weight							
	Reps							
	Weight							
	Reps							
	Weight							

Cardio	Duration	Distance	Heart Rate	Calories

Measurements

Neck	R Bicep	Chest	Waist	Hips	R Thigh	L Thigh	Calf

Note	

Date				Start Time			
Muscle Group				Finish Time			
Weight				Upper Body			
Lower Body				Abs			

Exercise	Sets	Set 1	Set 2	Set 3	Set 4	Set 5	Set 6	Set 7
	Reps							
	Weight							
	Reps							
	Weight							
	Reps							
	Weight							
	Reps							
	Weight							
	Reps							
	Weight							
	Reps							
	Weight							
	Reps							
	Weight							
	Reps							
	Weight							
	Reps							
	Weight							

Cardio	Duration	Distance	Heart Rate	Calories

Measurements								
Neck	R Bicep	Chest	Waist	Hips	R Thigh	L Thigh	Calf	

Note	

Date				Start Time				
Muscle Group				Finish Time				
Weight				Upper Body				
Lower Body				Abs				

Exercise	Sets	Set 1	Set 2	Set 3	Set 4	Set 5	Set 6	Set 7
	Reps							
	Weight							
	Reps							
	Weight							
	Reps							
	Weight							
	Reps							
	Weight							
	Reps							
	Weight							
	Reps							
	Weight							
	Reps							
	Weight							
	Reps							
	Weight							
	Reps							
	Weight							

Cardio	Duration	Distance	Heart Rate	Calories

Measurements

Neck	R Bicep	Chest	Waist	Hips	R Thigh	L Thigh	Calf

Note	

Date			Start Time	
Muscle Group			Finish Time	
Weight			Upper Body	
Lower Body			Abs	

Exercise	Sets	Set 1	Set 2	Set 3	Set 4	Set 5	Set 6	Set 7
	Reps							
	Weight							
	Reps							
	Weight							
	Reps							
	Weight							
	Reps							
	Weight							
	Reps							
	Weight							
	Reps							
	Weight							
	Reps							
	Weight							
	Reps							
	Weight							
	Reps							
	Weight							

Cardio	Duration	Distance	Heart Rate	Calories

Measurements

Neck	R Bicep	Chest	Waist	Hips	R Thigh	L Thigh	Calf

Note

World of Women Galaxy
WoWG #20449
The photo on the cover represents
an NFT from the World of Women
Galaxy collection.
I own this NFT and therefore the Intellectual Property rights.

Thank you!

www.ingramcontent.com/pod-product-compliance
Lightning Source LLC
LaVergne TN
LVHW011946070526
838202LV00054B/4820